Famous Restaurant Recipes
Copycat Versions of America's Favorite Restaurant Dishes

To my family

Published by Lulu Press, Inc.
www.lulu.com

ISBN 978-1-4116-9709-6

Cover Design by Sallie Stone through Lulu Press, Inc.
Interior Design by Sallie Stone.
Edited by Thomas Newbill.

Visit us on the web!
www.restaurantrecipesbook.com

Menu
(Copycat Restaurant Recipes)

1

Desserts:

Restaurant Recipes

The creation of this book began in the mid 1990's while I was working at Mozzarella's Cafe® (now The American Cafe®) as a waitress. The restaurant gave a generous employee discount, so I was able to sample many of their dishes. After stopping work there, I had cravings for their Italian Pie (now called Original New York Pasta Pie®) so I decided to recreate the dish at home. I knew the ingredients of the dish from reading the menu and eating it countless times. I made it at home for myself and my family. It turned out very close to the original. I also made their house salad and bread service at home too.

A few years later while browsing through a bookstore, I came upon a restaurant recipes cookbook. The book called *Top Secret Restaurant Recipes®: Creating Kitchen Clones from America's Favorite Restaurant Chains* by Todd Wilbur allowed me to make more restaurant dishes at home.

About 5 years after purchasing Wilbur's book, I decided to write my own. Some recipes were more challenging, while others were easier to create because there was a wealth of standard recipes to draw inspiration from. The recipes in my book are the result of years of experimenting. My family enjoys them and I believe your family will also.

Blank pages have been added at the end for you to fill in recipes from popular restaurants that post their recipes on the web.

Here is a list of some websites where you can find recipes to add:

www.benihana.com
www.ruthschris-sanantonio.com
www.olivegarden.com
www.redlobster.com

Also visit the companion website for more listings of restaurants that post their recipes, and to shop for restaurant recipes related products.

www.restaurantrecipesbook.com

I hope you enjoy cooking from this book and visiting the companion website.

Sallie Stone
May 2006

Orange Julius® Orange Julius® Copycat Restaurant Recipe
3 servings

Ingredients:
½ of 6 ounce can (1/3 cup) frozen orange juice concentrate
½ cup evaporated milk
½ cup water
1/4 cup sugar
½ teaspoon vanilla
6 ice cubes

Preparation:
Combine all ingredients in a blender. Cover and blend until smooth. (About 30 seconds).

Bill's Barbecue Limeade
Copycat Restaurant Recipe
5 servings

Bill's Barbecue is a small unit chain located in Richmond, Virginia.

Limeade
1 cup fresh lime juice (about 7 limes)
4 cups cold water
1 cup sugar
ice cubes
lime slices (1 lime)
mini juicer

Preparation:
Combine lime juice and water in a large pitcher. Add sugar; stir until well dissolved. Add more sugar to taste if desired. Pour into glasses with ice cubes. Garnish with one lime slice for each glass.

Applebee's® Shirley Temple
Copycat Restaurant Recipe
1 serving

Shirley Temple
8 ounces Sprite®
1 tablespoon grenadine syrup
maraschino cherry
straw
ice

Preparation:
Combine Sprite® and grenadine in a glass. Stir. Fill with ice. Place a straw in the glass and garnish with a cherry.

Roy Rogers:
Just substitute 8 ounces of Coke® for the 8 ounces of Sprite® in the above recipe.

Starbucks® Frappuccino®
Copycat Restaurant Recipe
2 servings

This recipe is for the bottled version of a Starbucks® Frappuccino®.

3 ounces instant expresso, chilled (Medaglia D'Oro Instant Expresso Coffee)
15 ounces low-fat milk
3/4 tablespoon dry pectin (optional)
2 tablespoons + 2 teaspoons sugar or sugar to taste

Preparation:
Brew 3 ounces expresso or make 3 ounces expresso made with instant expresso. Chill the coffee. Pour into a pitcher, add milk, sugar and pectin. Stir well. (Pectin is a thickener, that will make your drink creamier. It can be found in the canning section of your local supermarket.)

Variations: To make the mocha variety add a pinch of cocoa powder. You can also make the vanilla variety by adding a little vanilla extract to taste. Or to make this version with less calories use a sugar substitute instead of sugar.

Tip: Expresso ice cubes will save time in the above recipe. Pour 1 tablespoon (½ ounce) chilled expresso into each compartment of an ice cube tray and freeze a day ahead.

Store ice cubes in resealable plastic bags till ready to use. When making a Frappuccino® add two ice cubes to 2 ounces of expresso to make 3 ounces chilled expresso.

You can purchase instant expresso at:
www.amazon.com/gourmet

The American Cafe® Orange Spice Tea
Copycat Restaurant Recipe
6 servings

Orange Spice Tea
package of Lipton orange spice tea
1 orange, cut into 6 slices for garnish
ice
sugar
ice tea spoons
water

Preparation:
Brew the tea according to package directions. Pour tea into a pitcher, add water and stir. Cut the orange in half. Then face the orange down and cut three slices from each half. Cut a 1/4 inch slit down the middle of each orange slice and place one on the rim of each glass filled with ice and tea. Place an ice tea spoon in each glass.

Red Lobster Cheddar Bay Biscuits
Copycat Restaurant Recipe
Makes a dozen biscuits

Cheddar Bay Biscuits
2 cups Bisquick®
2/3 cup milk
½ cup sharp or white cheddar cheese, shredded
1/4 cup butter, melted
1 garlic clove minced or 1/4 teaspoon garlic powder
1 teaspoon parsley flakes

Preparation:
Melt butter over low heat. Add minced garlic and saute the garlic or add garlic powder without sauteing. Remove from heat and set aside. Add parsley to the garlic butter and stir. In a mixing bowl, mix together baking mix, milk and cheese until a soft dough forms, then beat vigorously 30 seconds. Drop from a spoon onto ungreased baking sheet and bake at 450 degrees F until golden brown, 8 to 10 minutes. Brush garlic butter over hot biscuits and serve hot.

The American Cafe® Bread Service
Copycat Restaurant Recipe
6 servings

loaf of Italian bread
Boursin cheese
ramekin(s)

Preparation:
Heat the bread, and place on a bread board. Cut the bread diagonally. Place Boursin cheese in ramekin(s) and spread on bread slices at the table.

Note: You can find Boursin cheese in the gourmet cheese section of your local supermarket.

Chili's® Skillet Queso
Copycat Restaurant Recipe
4 servings

Menu Description - "Our appetizing cheese dip with seasoned beef. Served with warm tostada chips."

Skillet Queso
1 pound Kraft® Velveeta® Cheese
1 can Hormel® No-Bean Chili
1 dash chili powder
1 bag tostada chips

Preparation:
Heat cheese in a medium saucepan over medium heat. After the cheese is melted stir in chili powder. Then stir in no-bean chili and heat through. Serve with lightly heated tostada chips. Bake chips for 3 minutes in a 250 degree F oven in a large baking dish.

Bennigan's® Irish Haystack
Copycat Restaurant Recipe
3 servings

Menu Description - "Thinly sliced onions, battered, fried and seasoned to perfection. Creamy Ranch dressing served on the side."

Irish Haystack
1 red onion
Chuck Wagon® Onion Ring mix
ranch dressing

Preparation:
Remove the skin from the onion, and slice into thin onion rings. Follow the directions on the onion ring mix box to prepare. Fry. Drain fried onion rings on paper towels. Serve with ranch dressing on the side.

Black-eyed Pea® Fried Corn
Copycat Restaurant Recipe
12 servings

Adapted from Pillsbury Fruits and Vegetables Cookbook.

Fried Corn
oil for deep frying
3/4 cup corn meal
½ cup grated Parmesan cheese
1/3 cup flour
3/4 teaspoon garlic salt
3/4 cup milk
2 tablespoons oil
1 egg
2 packages Green Giant® Nibblers® Frozen Corn-on-the-Cob, thawed
1 cup cornflake crumbs or crushed corn flakes

Preparation:
In a fryer or heavy saucepan, heat oil to 375 degrees F. Combine cornmeal, Parmesan cheese, flour, garlic salt, milk, oil and egg in a large bowl. Mix well. Dip corn-on-the-cob ears into cornmeal batter to coat; then roll in crushed cornflakes. Fry in hot oil 2 to 3 minutes or until lightly golden brown. Drain on paper towels. Serve immediately.

Outback Steakhouse® Sautéed 'Shrooms
Copycat Restaurant Recipe
6 servings

An excellent side dish to serve with your steak.

Burgundy Mushrooms
3 (8 ounce cans or jars whole mushrooms), drained
1 cup butter, melted
1/4 teaspoon pepper
½ teaspoon garlic powder
1 teaspoon beef bouillon
½ cup onion, chopped
1 cup Burgundy wine

Preparation:
Saute onions in butter for 5 minutes. Add mushrooms, cook for 25 minutes. Add Burgundy wine, pepper, garlic and beef bouillon. Simmer 20 minutes.

Black-eyed Pea® Glazed Carrots
Copycat Restaurant Recipe
5 servings

An excellent side dish to serve with a veggie platter and homemade cornbread or parker house rolls.

Glazed Carrots
1 pound baby carrots
1/4 cup orange juice
3 tablespoons brown sugar
2 tablespoons butter
pinch of salt

Preparation:
Place carrots in a medium saucepan, and cover with water. Boil until tender, drain in colander. Place carrots back in pan, and pour orange juice over them. Mix, and simmer over medium heat for about 5 minutes. Stir in brown sugar, butter, and salt. Heat until butter and sugar are melted.

The American Cafe® House (side salad)
Copycat Restaurant Recipe
1 serving

Menu Description - "Fresh salad greens, tomatoes, jack and cheddar cheeses, almonds and croutons."

Side Salad
1 ½ cups mixed salad greens
1/4 Roma tomato, diced
2 ½ tablespoons jack and cheddar cheese
1 ½ tablespoons sliced almonds
4 to 5 croutons

Preparation:
Place salad greens in a salad bowl. Top with diced tomatoes, cheeses, almonds and croutons. Serve with salad dressing.

Olive Garden® Tuscan Potatoes
Copycat Restaurant Recipe
4 servings

Serve this tasty side dish with your Pork Filettino.

Tuscan Potatoes
1 ½ pounds russet potatoes
4 tablespoons extra virgin olive oil
8 garlic cloves, minced
2 tablespoons fresh rosemary, chopped
1/8 teaspoon salt
1/8 teaspoon pepper

Preparation:
Preheat oven to 450 degrees F. Wash and dry potatoes, and cut them into wedges. Combine oil garlic, rosemary, salt and pepper in a small bowl. Toss potatoes with the oil and seasoning mixture. Transfer coated potatoes to a roasting pan. Cook for 25 to 30 minutes. Shake pan occasionally for even roasting. Remove from oven. Check the seasoning of salt and pepper to taste. Sprinkle additional salt and pepper lightly and evenly over potatoes if desired.

The American Cafe® California Bleu
Copycat Restaurant Recipe
1 serving

Menu Description - "Fresh mixed greens topped with Bleu Cheese crumbles, spicy sugared walnuts and fresh strawberries. Served with Bleu cheese toast and Sweet Balsamic Vinaigrette dressing."

California Bleu
1 ½ cups mixed greens
2 teaspoons bleu cheese crumbles
1 ½ tablespoons spicy sugared walnuts, chopped
2 strawberries, sliced
4 to 5 croutons
Balsamic Vinaigrette

Preparation:
Mix together above ingredients. Place in a salad bowl. Drizzle balsamic vinaigrette over salad.

Spicy Sugared Walnuts
2 cups walnut halves
3/4 cup sugar
1/4 cup water
1 teaspoon cinnamon (optional)

Preparation:
Lightly grease a baking sheet. In a one quart microwave safe glass measure, combine walnut

halves, sugar, cinnamon and water. Cook in microwave oven on high setting for 8 to 8 ½ minutes, or until sugar has caramelized. Stir several times during cooking. Pour out onto prepared baking sheet, and separate into pieces. Let cool completely.

7 servings

Bleu Cheese Walnut Toast

1 loaf French baguette, cut into 1/3 inch slices
1/4 cup butter, melted
4 ounces crumbled bleu cheese
1/4 cup butter, softened
salt and pepper to taste
½ cup chopped walnuts
½ cup fresh parsley, chopped

Preparation:

Preheat the oven to 400 degrees F.
Brush one side each of bread with melted butter, and place butter side up on a baking sheet. Bake for 7 minutes, or until lightly toasted.
In a bowl, combine the bleu cheese, softened butter, salt and pepper. Spread this mixture over the tops of the toasted bread slices, and sprinkle with chopped walnuts.
Bake for 6 minutes in the oven, or until the topping is melted and bubbly. Arrange on a serving plate and sprinkle with chopped parsley.

Outback Steakhouse® Roasted Garlic Mashed Potatoes
Copycat Restaurant Recipe
4 servings

Roasted Garlic Mashed Potatoes

3 large Russet potatoes, peeled and quartered
1 head of garlic
2 tablespoons unsalted butter
½ cup milk
1/4 cup buttermilk
2 tablespoons olive oil
1 ½ teaspoons dried thyme
salt and pepper to taste

Preparation:

Peel the outer skin of the garlic leaving garlic cloves whole. Place the garlic cloves in a baking dish. Drizzle with oil making sure to coat all the garlic. Sprinkle with the dried thyme. Bake at 350 degrees f covered with tinfoil for 20 to 30 minutes, or until tender and golden brown.

Peel and cut potatoes into four portions each. Boil in salted water for 20 to 30 minutes, or until tender. Meanwhile heat the milk, buttermilk and butter in saucepan. When the potatoes are done drain and return them to the same pot. Slowly add the milk and butter while mashing with a potato masher until desired consistency is achieved; add garlic to taste. Stir well. Season mashed potatoes with salt and pepper to taste.

Ruby Tuesday's® Coconut Shrimp
Copycat Restaurant Recipe
4 servings

Menu Description - "Crispy coconut shrimp with sweet and hot ginger dipping sauce. Served with broccoli and brown rice pilaf topped with cheese and tomatoes."

Fried Coconut Shrimp
1 cup shredded sweetened coconut
1 cup bread crumbs
dash of salt
dash of freshly ground pepper
1 cup all-purpose flour
2 large eggs, beaten
36 large shrimp, peeled and de-veined
vegetable oil, for frying

Preparation:
In large bowl, mix coconut, bread crumbs, salt and pepper. Place flour, eggs, and bread crumb mixture into 3 separate bowls. Dredge the shrimp in flour and shake off excess. Next, dip the shrimp thoroughly in the egg and rub against the side of the bowl to lightly remove excess. Finally, coat the shrimp thoroughly with the bread crumb mixture. Lay out the shrimp on a plate until ready to fry. Heat one inch of oil to 350 degrees F. Fry the shrimp in batches until golden brown and cooked through, about 3 to 4 minutes per batch. Drain on paper

towels.

Sweet and Hot Ginger Dipping Sauce
1 cup orange marmalade
2 tablespoons orange juice
2 tablespoons lemon juice
1 teaspoon dry mustard
2 teaspoons horseradish
1 small piece ginger, pressed

Preparation:
Press the ginger in a garlic press. Combine
marmalade, orange and lemon juices in a food
processor. Mix in remaining ingredients. Chill. May
be stored in refrigerator
for up to two weeks.

Steak and Ale® Rosemary Chicken
Copycat Restaurant Recipe
2 servings

Adapted from Cooking Light Magazine August 2005.

Rosemary Chicken
2 chicken breast, butterflied
1/4 teaspoon kosher salt (first step)
1/4 teaspoon kosher salt (second step)
1 garlic clove, minced
1/8 teaspoon freshly ground pepper
1 tablespoon fresh rosemary, chopped
1 teaspoon olive oil
cooking spray

Preparation:
Combine rosemary, oil, salt and garlic. Rub mixture evenly over both sides of chicken. Cover and marinate for 3 hours in the refrigerator. Remove from the refrigerator. Sprinkle both sides of chicken with pepper and an additional 1/4 teaspoon of kosher salt. Lightly oil the grill plate. Grill.

Ruby Tuesday's® Memphis Dry Rub Ribs
Copycat Restaurant Recipe
3 servings

Menu description - "Hang Off The Plate Ribs® A colossal portion of fork-tender premium baby back ribs. Slow-cooked for hours and seasoned with our secret spices. They've got attitude!"

Adapted from BBQ USA: 425 FIERY RECIPES FROM ALL ACROSS AMERICA.

Memphis Dry Rub Ribs
2 tablespoons paprika
1 tablespoon black pepper
1 tablespoon dark brown sugar
1 ½ teaspoons salt
1 ½ teaspoons celery salt
1 teaspoon garlic powder
1 teaspoon dry mustard
1 teaspoon cumin
1/4 teaspoon cayenne pepper
pinch of onion powder
1 rack of baby back ribs
Stubb's MOPPIN' SAUCE BAR-B-Q BASTE
basting brush

Preparation:
Mix all dry ingredients in a bowl. Rub 2/3 of the mixture onto front and back of ribs. Lightly brush on barbecue sauce. Grill. Sprinkle remaining Rub onto

top of ribs after grilling.

Red Lobster® Apple Walnut Chicken Salad
Copycat Restaurant Recipe
2 servings

Menu Description - "Grilled marinated chicken over mixed greens, red bell peppers, sun-dried tomatoes, bleu cheese, apple & walnuts, with a balsamic vinaigrette."

Apple Walnut Chicken Salad
2 chicken breasts marinated in balsamic vinaigrette
5 cups mixed greens
1 red delicious apple, cored and un-peeled cut into bite sized pieces and tossed with one teaspoon lemon juice to prevent browning
5 tablespoons chopped walnuts
2 tablespoons sun-dried tomatoes, chopped
4 teaspoons crumbled bleu cheese
1/4 red bell pepper, diced
croutons
2 bottles of balsamic vinaigrette salad dressing

Preparation:
Marinate the chicken in balsamic vinaigrette for one hour in a resealable plastic bag in the refrigerator. Grill or bake the chicken until done. Cut into strips. Toss salads in two separate bowls, mix in walnuts, sun-dried tomatoes, bleu cheese and red bell pepper. Place grilled chicken strips over each salad. Place croutons on each salad. Drizzle salad dressing over each salad at the table.

Chili's® Guiltless Black Bean Burger
Copycat Restaurant Recipe
4 servings

Menu Description - "Our meatless black bean patty topped with low fat ranch, shredded lettuce, tomato, pickle and onion."

Black Bean Burger
1 ½ cans black beans (16 ounces each can with one can halved or 24 ounces total), rinsed and drained
2 tablespoons chopped white onion
1/4 cup or 4 tablespoons diced red bell pepper
½ teaspoon cayenne pepper
about ½ of an egg
about ½ cup bread crumbs
1 tablespoon fresh cilantro or parsley, chopped
1 tablespoon olive oil or vegetable oil

Sandwich
4 gourmet wheat hamburger buns
low fat ranch dressing
shredded ice-berg lettuce
tomato
pickles
red onion

Preparation:
Mix one egg in a bowl. Use half of the mixture in the next step. Combine black beans, onion, bell pepper, cayenne, egg, bread crumbs and cilantro or parsley

in food processor and blend. If the mixture is not dry enough to shape, add more bread crumbs. Form and shape into four patties. For best results make 24 hours ahead and refrigerate so patties will set well. Heat 1 tablespoon olive oil in large frying pan over medium heat. Fry the patties 2 minutes each side. Arrange sandwich with patty, low fat ranch dressing, red onion, pickles and one slice of tomato for each sandwich.

Note: Fresh not dried cilantro or parsley work best in this recipe.

Making Bread Crumbs Tip: Cut fresh bread into cubes. Place them on a baking sheet and bake at 350 degrees F until crisp, about 15 to 20 minutes. Process the cubes in a blender or food processor until finely ground.

Red Lobster® Grilled Rainbow Trout with Citrus Butter
Copycat Restaurant Recipe
2 servings

Menu Description - "Flame-grilled & topped with a citrus butter. Served with a side salad, seasonal vegetables & your choice of side."

Citrus Butter
½ cup unsalted butter, melted
4 teaspoons fresh lemon juice
4 teaspoons fresh orange juice
2 dashes of salt
2 dashes of paprika

Trout
2 trout fillets

Tool:
1 basting brush for sauce

Preparation:
Combine all ingredients except trout in a small saucepan over low heat and cook until butter is melted. Remove from heat. Set aside citrus butter in two ramekins. Brush remaining citrus butter over trout. Grill. Continue to brush sauce over trout during grilling. Serve hot.

36

O'Charley's® Black & Bleu Caesar Salad
Copycat Restaurant Recipe
2 servings

Menu Description - "Hearts of romaine topped with blackened sirloin, Roma tomatoes, crisp bacon and crumbled bleu cheese. Tossed with our Caesar dressing."

Blackened Sirloin
2 (6 ounce) sirloin steaks, cut into strips after cooking
4 teaspoons blackened steak seasoning
½ cup butter, melted

Preparation:
Dip steak into butter. Either rub blackened steak seasoning on each side of steak, or generously and evenly sprinkle seasoning on each side. Grill steak to desired doneness.

Salad
5 cups romaine lettuce
6 slices Roma tomato
4 slices cooked bacon, crumbled into two servings
4 teaspoons crumbled bleu cheese
2 tablespoons Parmesan cheese, shredded
croutons
Caesar dressing

Preparation:

Place 2 ½ cups of romaine in a bowl. Add two slices bacon crumbled, 1 tablespoon shredded Parmesan cheese, and two teaspoons crumbled bleu cheese. Toss. Transfer to a serving bowl. Place sirloin strips and three Roma tomato slices on salad. Drizzle with Caesar dressing and garnish with croutons. Repeat.

Tip: To serve the salad the way the restaurant does, toss the lettuce with Caesar dressing, adding a little dressing at a time to taste. Do this before adding toppings. Toss again after adding toppings before placing steak, tomatoes and croutons on salad.

Hooter's® HOOTER's WINGS
Copycat Restaurant Recipe

Menu Description - "NEARLY WORLD FAMOUS OFTEN IMITATED, HARDLY EVER DUPLICATED. SHAKEN IN MILD, MEDIUM, HOT, MILE ISLAND, 911 CAJUN, SAMURAI, or SPICY JACK WING SAUCE."

Wings
Hooter's® Wing Breading Mix
Hooter's® Wing Sauce
package buffalo wing pieces

On the side
carrots, cut into sticks
celery, cut into sticks
bleu cheese or ranch dressing

Note: Hooter's® products can be found in the condiments isle of your local supermarket.

Bennigan's® Reuben
Copycat Restaurant Recipe
1 serving

Menu Description - "Delicious, warm corned beef, thinly sliced and topped with fresh sauerkraut and white cheddar and Swiss cheeses. Served on toasted potato rye bread with Thousand Island dressing."

Reuben
6 thinly sliced slices corned beef
2 tablespoons fresh sauerkraut, drained
thin slice white cheddar
thin slice Swiss cheese
2 slices potato rye bread or regular rye bread
1 tablespoon butter or margarine
thousand island dressing, on the side

Preparation:
Butter one side each slice of potato rye bread. Place them butter side down in a frying pan. Set temperature to low heat. Place cheeses on one slice, corned beef on the other, topped with drained sauerkraut. Grill the slices to golden brown. Remove from heat. Place the slice with corned beef and sauerkraut on a plate. Place the slice with cheese on top of the sauerkraut. Serve with thousand island dressing on the side.

Benihana® Vegetable Delight (Tsutsumi - Yaki) Copycat Restaurant Recipe
1 serving

Menu Description - "Served with Teriyaki Tofu appetizer, Japanese noodles, assorted vegetables with seasonings, wrapped and cooked on the grill."

Adapted from www.benihana.com

Vegetable Delight
1 ounce fresh boiled potato, diced
5 slices mushroom
1 ounce zucchini, sliced
1 ounce fresh snap beans, boiled
salt and pepper
1 teaspoon oil
1 ounce fresh cooked carrot, sliced
2 ounces sliced onion
2 ounces fresh boiled broccoli
6 water chestnuts
1 teaspoon white wine
1/4 lime
1 teaspoon butter
rice paper

Preparation:
Coat one side of square foot of damp rice paper with oil and butter. Combine remaining ingredients with 2 teaspoons water; place ingredients in rice paper and wrap tightly. Cook three and a half minutes in

heated non-stick skillet. Cook another three and half minutes on other side until paper expands. Place paper on plate and cut open with scissors. Be careful: air inside paper is very hot.

Note: The lime adds flavor through the steam. Do not squeeze the lime to make juice.

Olive Garden® Pork Filettino
Copycat Restaurant Recipe
4 servings

Menu Description - "Grilled pork tenderloin marinated in extra-virgin olive oil and rosemary. Served with Tuscan potatoes and bell peppers."

Pork Filettino
1 pork tenderloin
2 tablespoons extra-virgin olive oil or rosemary infused olive oil without adding rosemary
1 tablespoon fresh garlic, minced
1 tablespoon fresh rosemary, chopped
1/8 teaspoon salt
1/8 teaspoon black pepper
1/4 package prepared or jar prepared veal demi-glacé

Preparation:
Sprinkle tenderloin with salt and pepper on all sides. Brush with mixture of olive oil, rosemary and garlic. Marinate for approximately two hours. Grill until internal temperature of pork reaches 165 degrees F. Remove from heat. Heat demi-glacé and pour over pork. Garnish with fresh rosemary if desired.

The American Cafe® Roasted Garlic Alfredo
Copycat Restaurant Recipe
2 servings

Menu Description - "Fettuccine tossed in a rich, roasted garlic cream sauce with Parmesan Cheese."

Roasted Garlic Alfredo
½ pound fettuccine, dry
1 ½ cup cream
3/4 cup Parmesan, grated
2 tablespoons roasted garlic, pureed
salt and pepper to taste

Preparation:
First roast the garlic. Cook the pasta until just tender. Drain and rinse. Set aside. Heat the cream in a skillet over medium heat. Whisk in the cheese and garlic. Reduce sauce slightly. Check seasonings. Toss in the cooked pasta. Serve warm.

Roasted Garlic
1 garlic head
1 teaspoon extra-virgin olive oil

Preparation:
Preheat the oven to 375 degrees F. Peel the outer skin of the garlic only; leave garlic bulb whole. Slice ½ - inch of the pointed end of the garlic bulb. Pour ½ teaspoon olive oil over the top bulb and let it sink

in between the cloves. Wait two minutes and then repeat with another ½ teaspoon of olive oil. Cover and bake one hour or until cloves are browned at the exposed end and soft throughout. Remove from oven. Allow garlic to cool. Remove cloves from head as needed. To puree, crush garlic cloves with the flat of a knife.

Olive Garden® Mushroom Alfredo
Copycat Restaurant Recipe
3 servings

Website Description - "A creamy alfredo sauce made with fresh mushrooms and a hint of garlic."

This dish is from the Olive Garden® Never Ending Pasta Bowls Menu. You can choose between seven different pastas for this particular menu: Whole Wheat Linguine, Spaghetti, Penne, Fettuccine, Linguine, Farfalle and Angel Hair.

Mushroom Alfredo
3/4 pound pasta
2 cups whipping cream
3/4 cup Parmesan, grated
3 tablespoons butter
1 teaspoon garlic powder
2 ½ cups mushrooms, sliced
1 tablespoon margarine

Preparation:
Saute sliced mushrooms in one tablespoon of melted margarine over low heat until golden brown. Pour whipping cream into a medium saucepan while pasta is cooking in another pan. Cook over medium heat. Stir in cheese slowly, whisking until blended. Whisk in butter. Remove from heat. Continue beating until sauce thickens. Season with garlic powder, stirring well. Stir in mushrooms or reserve to divide among

46

plates. Serve sauce hot over pasta with mushrooms on top. Season the entree with pepper at the table if desired.

Applebee's® Crispy Buttermilk Shrimp
Copycat Restaurant Recipe
3 servings

Menu Description - "A heaping platter of shrimp, lightly breaded and fried to perfection. Served with garlic mashed potatoes, fresh seasonal vegetables, garlic toast and cocktail dipping sauce."

Crispy Buttermilk Shrimp
1 pound raw large shrimp, de-veined
1 cup flour
1 cup cornflakes, crushed
1 cup buttermilk
1/4 teaspoon salt
1/4 teaspoon pepper
oil

Preparation:
Mix together cornflakes and buttermilk. Dip shrimp into wet batter. Mix flour, salt and pepper together in a bowl. Transfer flour mixture to a resealable plastic bag. Then place 6 shrimp at a time in the flour mixture and shake gently. Place shrimp on a plate to reserve for frying. Fry until golden brown on each side in 400 degree F one inch hot oil.

Cocktail Sauce
1 cup ketchup
2 teaspoons prepared horseradish
½ teaspoon Worcestershire

3 drops red pepper sauce

Preparation:
Combine all ingredients in a bowl. Chill.

Tip: Homemade buttermilk is less expensive than store bought buttermilk and is easy to make. Add one teaspoon distilled white vinegar to one cup fresh milk; let sour for 5 minutes.

Houlihan's® Chcken BLT on Focaccia
Copycat Restaurant Recipe
1 serving

Menu Description - "Freshly baked Focaccia bread with marinated chicken, smoked bacon, lettuce and tomato."

Chcken BLT
package of Focaccia Italian Herbs and Cheese or
Rosemary bread
bottle of Italian dressing
1 chicken breast
3 strips of bacon, cooked and drained
iceberg lettuce
tomato slice
mayonnaise

Preparation:
Marinate the chicken breast in Italian dressing for 1 hour by pouring dressing into a resealable plastic bag with chicken. Refrigerate.
Make Focaccia bread according to package directions. Allow bread to cool on a wire rack. Then cut two slices large enough to place chicken in between slices.
Grill or bake chicken.
Arrange the sandwich by placing chicken on the bottom slice, bacon, lettuce then tomato. Spread top slice of bread with mayonnaise if desired.

O'Charley's® Pecan Chicken Tender Salad
Copycat Restaurant Recipe
4 servings

Menu Description - "Pecan-encrusted chicken served warm on a bed of crisp romaine lettuce with mandarin oranges, crumbled bleu cheese, dried cranberries and honey roasted Georgia pecans. Served with our Balsamic Vinaigrette."

Pecan Tenders
vegetable oil, for frying
2 pounds chicken tenders
salt and pepper
1 cup flour
2 eggs, beaten with a splash of milk
1 cup plain bread crumbs
1 cup pecans, processed in food processor to finely chop
½ teaspoon nutmeg, ground
1 tablespoon orange juice

Preparation:
Heat one inch of oil over medium heat. Season chicken tenders with salt and pepper. Set out three dishes. In the first dish, place the flour. In the second, eggs beaten with milk. In the third dish, combine bread crumbs, ground pecans, nutmeg and orange juice. Coat tenders in flour, then egg, then pecan mixture. Place tenders on a plate to reserve for frying. Fry in batches 3 to 3 ½ minutes per side.

51

Drain on paper towels.

Honey Roasted Pecans
1/4 cup honey
1 teaspoon salt
2 cups pecans

Preparation:
Heat oven to 350 degrees F. Stir together honey salt, then add pecans, tossing to coat well. Spread pecans in one layer in a shallow baking pan. Bake for 15 minutes. Then stir pecans and bake for 3 to 5 minutes more. Working quickly, transfer to wax paper sheet to cool. While the pecans are still warm separate them with a fork. Once they are cool chop pecans if desired.

Salad
romaine lettuce
mandarin orange slices
crumbled bleu cheese
dried cranberries
balsamic vinaigrette

Preparation:
In separate bowls mix together all ingredients except tenders and dressing. For every serving toss together 2 ½ cups of lettuce, 2 teaspoons crumbled bleu cheese, 2 teaspoons dried cranberries, 2 ½ tablespoons chopped honey roasted pecans and two mandarin orange slices cut in half. Place tenders on

top of salad. Drizzle dressing on salads at the table.

Waffle House® Pecan Waffle
Copycat Restaurant Recipe
6 servings

Pecan Waffles
2 cups baking mix, such as Bisquick®
1 cup milk
1 egg
2 tablespoons vegetable oil
1/4 cup finely chopped pecans
syrup or Reddi whip®

Preparation:
Stir ingredients until well blended. Pour batter into greased waffle iron. Close the waffle iron to bake. Serve with Reddi whip® on top of waffle or with syrup.

Variation: To make Banana - Nut Waffles add 1 cup mashed very ripe banana. (About 2 bananas). Also try Banana - Nut Waffles with finely chopped walnuts instead of pecans.

Burger King® Chicken Fries
Copycat Restaurant Recipe
4 servings

Chicken Fries
1 package boneless skinless chicken breasts
½ cup flour
½ cup Zatarain's® Wonderful Fish-Fri
1 egg
oil
meat scissors
barbecue sauce or honey mustard dressing for dipping

Preparation:
Butterfly the chicken breasts. Then cut them down the middle to separate the breast halves. Next cut into the shape of chicken fries with meat scissors or a knife. Put flour and Fish Fri into separate resealable plastic bags. Lightly beat the egg with one tablespoon water. Shake four chicken fries at a time in the flour, shake off the excess, dip in egg wash, shake off the excess, then shake in Fish Fri. Place each chicken fry on a plate to reserve for frying. Heat one inch of oil in a skillet to medium hot. Fry chicken fries in batches so they do not touch, turning, until they are golden brown. Drain chicken fries on paper towels and serve.

Red Lobster® Jumbo Parrot Bay Coconut Shrimp
Copycat Restaurant Recipe
4 servings

Menu Description - "Dipped in batter flavored with Captain Morgan Parrot Bay Rum & coconut flakes. Served with piña colada dipping sauce."

Adapted from www.recipezaar.com.

Coconut Shrimp
canola oil for fryer
24 large shrimp, peeled and de-veined
1 ½ cups all-purpose flour, divided
2 tablespoons sugar
1/4 teaspoon salt
1 cup milk
2 tablespoons Captain Morgan Parrot Bay Coconut Rum
1 cup bread crumbs
½ cup shredded sweetened coconut

Preparation:
Heat oil to 350 degrees F.
Measure 3/4 cup flour into a medium bowl.
In a second, medium bowl combine, 3/4 cup flour, sugar and salt.
Stir rum and milk into flour mixture in the second bowl, let it stand for 5 minutes.
Combine breadcrumbs and shredded coconut into a third bowl.

56

Butterfly cut each shrimp before you start the battering. Use a sharp knife to slice through the top of the shrimp (where the vein was) so that you can spread the shrimp open.
Leave the tail intact.
To batter the shrimp, dip each one in the flour, then in the wet batter, then coat each shrimp with the bread crumb/coconut mixture.
Place shrimp on a plate to reserve for frying. Fry the shrimp by dropping six at a time into the hot oil for 2 to 3 minutes or until the shrimp are golden brown.
Drain on paper towels.
Serve with piña colada dipping sauce.

Adapted from www.robbiehaf.com.

Piña Colada Dipping Sauce
½ cup sour cream
1/4 cup piña colada nonalcoholic drink mix
1/4 cup crushed pineapple
sugar to taste

Preparation:
Mix all ingredients together. Chill.

Steak and Ale® Cedar Plank Salmon
Copycat Restaurant Recipe
4 servings

Menu Description - "Grilled on a cedar plank and topped with lemon buerre blanc. Served with asparagus spears."

Lemon Buerre Blanc
½ cup dry white wine
2 tablespoons chopped green onions
3 tablespoons lemon juice
2 teaspoons minced garlic
1 tablespoon minced shallots
10 tablespoons unsalted butter, cut into chunks
salt and white pepper to taste
1 tablespoon chopped fresh parsley

Salmon
4 salmon fillets

Preparation:
While the salmon is grilling, add the wine, green onions, lemon juice, garlic and shallots to a saucepan over medium heat. Cook the mixture for 8 to 10 minutes or until the liquid is reduced by half. Reduce the heat to low and whisk or stir in 6 tablespoons of the butter. Remove the saucepan from the heat and whisk in or stir in the remaining 4 tablespoons of the butter. Continue to whisk or stir the sauce. Season the sauce with salt and white

pepper to taste. Finally, pour the sauce through a fine mesh strainer. Top salmon with hot lemon buerre blanc and serve.

You can purchase a cedar plank for grilling at www.justsmokedsalmon.com

According to their website a cedar plank increases the food's juice retention while instilling a delightful wood smoked flavor.

Red Lobster® Crab Alfredo
Copycat Restaurant Recipe
4 servings

Menu Description - "Sweet crabmeat & linguini with a creamy Alfredo sauce."

Easy Crab Alfredo
1 (9 ounce) package prepared linguini
1 (10 ounce) package refrigerated Alfredo Sauce
8 ounces fresh lump crabmeat
1/4 cup shredded Parmesan cheese

Preparation:
Heat sauce and crabmeat in saucepan over medium heat; add pasta, heat through. Divide among 4 plates. Top with Parmesan.

Homemade Crab Alfredo
2 cups whipping cream
3/4 cup Parmesan, grated
2 tablespoons butter
1/4 teaspoon nutmeg or 1 teaspoon garlic powder
12 ounces lump crabmeat

Preparation:
Pour whipping cream into a medium saucepan. Cook over medium heat. Stir in cheese slowly, whisking until blended. Whisk in butter. Remove from heat. Continue beating until sauce thickens. Season with

nutmeg or garlic powder. Stir in lump crabmeat. Heat for additional 3 minutes while stirring occasionally. Serve hot over pasta.

Pasta
1 pound of linguini
5 tablespoons Parmesan, shredded for topping

Preparation:
Cook linguini according to package directions. Top pasta with Alfredo sauce and shredded Parmesan.

Gourmet Crab Alfredo
Substitute crab leg meat from 6 or so boiled crab legs for the lump crabmeat. Boil crab legs for 3 minutes only.

Tip: When boiling crab, add one tablespoon of vinegar to the water. This helps to loosen the meat from the shell.

Chili's® Margarita Grilled Chicken
Copycat Restaurant Recipe
4 servings

Menu Description - "We start with tender, juicy chicken breast, marinate it with our classic Margarita flavoring and grill it to perfection. Served with rice, black beans, tortilla strips & pico de gallo."

Margarita Grilled Chicken
4 boneless chicken breasts
2 ½ cups liquid margarita mix

Preparation:
Pour margarita mix into a resealable plastic bag. Place chicken breasts in bag. Marinate in the refrigerator for 8 hours. Lightly oil the grill plate with cooking spray. Grill chicken breasts. Serve hot.

Subway® Vinegar & Oil for Subs
Copycat Restaurant Recipe

The secret to not getting too much vinegar on your sandwich is to mix equal parts of vinegar and oil into a condiment squeeze bottle.

Vinegar & Oil
1 part red wine vinegar
1 part oil
condiment squeeze bottle

Preparation:
Measure out equal portions of red wine vinegar and oil into the condiment squeeze bottle. Shake well before each use. Refrigerate.

Condiment squeeze bottles can be purchased at:
www.cooking.com™

Steak and Ale® Garlic Sirloin
Copycat Restaurant Recipe
4 servings

Menu Description - "Seasoned with garlic and topped with homemade garlic butter."

Garlic Sirloin
½ cup butter
2 teaspoons garlic powder
6 garlic cloves, minced
4 sirloin steaks
salt and pepper to taste
basting brush

Preparation:
Lightly oil the grill plate with cooking spray. Preheat grill for high heat. In a small saucepan, melt butter over low heat with garlic powder and 4 cloves minced garlic. Set aside. Sprinkle both sides of each steak with salt and pepper. Sprinkle one side of each steak with the two garlic cloves, minced. Place meat on grill. Cook for 4 to 5 minutes per side or until desired doneness is achieved. When done, transfer to warmed plates. Brush tops liberally with garlic butter, and allow to rest for 2 minutes before serving.

Red Robin® BLTA CROISSANT
Copycat Restaurant Recipe
1 serving

Menu Description - "A buttery croissant filled with sliced turkey breast, hickory maple-smoked bacon, fresh sliced avocado, lettuce, tomatoes & mayo. Served with our bottomless steak fries."

BLTA Croissant
1 croissant
2 thinly sliced deli style turkey breast
4 slices hickory maple-smoked bacon
one layer iceberg lettuce
1 tomato slice
2 slices avocado
mayo

Preparation:
Cut open croissant, and place turkey on the bottom slice. Next add cooked and drained bacon slices. Heat in the oven if desired with aluminum foil wrapped around the sandwich. Remove from oven, and add one layer of lettuce, tomato and one layer of avocado. Spread mayo on the top slice of the croissant.

Steak and Ale® HAWAIIAN CHICKEN
Copycat Restaurant Recipe
4 servings

Menu Description - "Marinated in pineapple juice, soy sauce and sherry wine, grilled and served with rice pilaf."

Easy Hawaiian Chicken
4 chicken breasts
Lawry's® Teriyaki with pineapple juice 30 minute Marinade

Preparation:
Pour marinade in a large resealable plastic bag. Butterfly chicken breasts. Add chicken breasts to resealable bag. Marinate for 30 minutes in refrigerator. Grill. Serve.

Hawaiian Chicken Recipe
16 ounces unsweetened pineapple juice
2 ½ ounces soy sauce
2 ounces dry cooking sherry
3/4 cup sugar
½ teaspoon granulated garlic
1 can sliced pineapple
4 chicken breasts

Preparation:
Combine pineapple juice, soy sauce, sherry, sugar

and garlic. Reserve ½ cup marinade for grilling.
Marinate chicken in the refrigerator for 8 hours.
Brush meat with canola oil in order to seal in the
juices. Grill and baste occasionally with remaining
marinade. Place pineapple slices on the grill and
cook approximately 1 minute on each side until
lightly browned.
Place meat on a plate and garnish with pineapple.

Country Store Sausage - Cheese Balls
Copycat Restaurant Recipe
Makes 60 -70 balls

This recipe is after an appetizer sold in an old country store near my home. They are great for breakfast too.

Sausage - Cheese Balls
1 pound Jimmy Dean Hot Sausage
1 pound grated sharp cheddar cheese
3 cups Bisquick®
½ cup water

Preparation:
Heat oven to 375 degrees F. Place sausage, baking mix and cheese together in a big bowl and stir well or mix with your hands. If mix is too dry, add ½ cup water. Roll into one inch sized balls and place on a greased cookie sheet. Bake for 20 minutes. They should be golden brown and sausage cooked through.

Steak and Ale® KENSINGTON® CLUB
Copycat Restaurant Recipe
4 servings

Menu Description - "Certified Black Angus Sirloin. Marinated in pineapple juice, soy sauce and sherry wine."

Easy Hawaiian Steak
4 sirloin steaks
2 bottles Lawry's® Teriyaki with pineapple juice 30 Minute Marinade

Preparation:
Pour marinade in two resealable plastic bags. Add two sirloins to each bag. Marinate for 30 minutes in refrigerator. Grill. Serve.

Hawaiian Steak Recipe
16 ounces unsweetened pineapple juice
2 ½ ounces soy sauce
2 ounces dry cooking sherry
3/4 cup sugar
½ teaspoon granulated garlic
1 can sliced pineapple
4 sirloin steaks

Preparation:
Combine pineapple juice, soy sauce, sherry, sugar and garlic. Reserve ½ cup of marinade for grilling.

Marinate steak in remaining marinade in the refrigerator for 8 hours.
Brush meat with a canola oil in order to seal in the juices. Grill and baste with reserved marinade occasionally.
Place pineapple slices on grill and cook approximately 1 minute on each side until lightly browned. Place meat on a plate and garnish with pineapple.

Red Robin® THE BANZAI BURGER™
Copycat Restaurant Recipe
1 serving

Menu Description - "Marinated in teriyaki and topped with grilled pineapple, Cheddar cheese, lettuce, tomatoes and mayo. Dude, you'll be like, ready to ride the pipeline on O'ahu's North Shore after you chomp on this!"

Hawaiian Burger
quarter pound hamburger patty
Lawry's® Teriyaki with pineapple juice 30 Minute Marinade
1 thin slice cheddar cheese
lettuce
1 tomato slice
1 slice grilled pineapple
mayo

Preparation:
Form the hamburger into a patty. Next drizzle teriyaki in a baking dish. Place patty on top of the drizzled teriyaki. Then drizzle teriyaki on top of the burger. Cover and place in the refrigerator for 30 minutes to marinate. Lightly oil the grill plate and grill burger. (Or pan fry by placing salt in skillet first.) In the last stage of grilling place cheese on top of the burger and grill pineapple until warm and slightly browned. Or fry pineapple in pan sprayed with cooking spray on low heat. Assemble the burger

with burger on top of bottom bun, lettuce, tomato
and grilled pineapple. Spread top bun with
mayonnaise if desired.

The American Cafe® Original New York Pasta Pie®
Copycat Restaurant Recipe
2 servings

Menu Description - "Penne pasta tossed with marinara sauce and baked with pepperoni, Italian sausage, mushrooms, black olives, red and green peppers topped with mozzarella and Parmesan cheeses."

If you like pizza and pasta, you'll love this dish. It's up to you what toppings to include. The important step is to coat the penne with marinara before layering the pie.

Pasta Pie
2 cups cooked penne pasta
1 cup marinara
12 pepperoni slices
1 tablespoon Italian sausage, chopped and cooked
3 mushrooms, sliced and cut in half
12 black olive slices
1 teaspoon red bell pepper
1 teaspoon green bell pepper
1 cup + 1 teaspoon mozzarella cheese
9 ½ inch round baking dish
Parmesan cheese, shredded for garnish

Preparation:

Preheat oven to 350 degrees F. Boil penne according to package directions. Drain in a colander. Transfer to a large mixing bowl. Add 1 cup of marinara sauce. Mix well. In a 9 ½ inch round baking dish place marinara coated penne pasta. Then sprinkle 1 cup of mozzarella on top of penne. Add toppings except pepperoni. Then add a layer of pepperoni. Sprinkle top layer of pepperoni with one teaspoon of mozzarella. Bake for 30 minutes until cheese is lightly browned and bubbly. Garnish with shredded Parmesan for best results.

Olive Garden® Capellini Pomodoro
Copycat Restaurant Recipe
4 servings

Menu Description - "Roma tomatoes, garlic, fresh basil and extra-virgin olive oil tossed with capellini."

Capellini Pomodoro
2 garlic cloves, minced
2 pounds Roma tomatoes, diced
1 ounce fresh basil leaves, minced
1/3 cup extra-virgin olive oil
3 ounces Parmesan cheese, shredded
12 ounces capellini pasta, cooked
1/8 teaspoon pepper
1/8 teaspoon salt

Preparation:
Heat olive oil and add garlic. Sautée garlic until it turns white. Add tomatoes, pepper and salt and heat through. Stir constantly for about 2 to 3 minutes. Check the seasoning of salt and pepper to taste. Remove from heat. Transfer hot cooked pasta to a large bowl. Toss pasta with tomato mixture and basil. Serve immediately and top with shredded Parmesan for best results.

Applebee's® Club House Grill
Copycat Restaurant Recipe
1 serving

Menu Description - "Served warm with sliced ham and oven-roasted turkey. Topped with Jack & cheddar cheeses, savory bacon, lettuce and tomato. Served on grilled sourdough with mayo and Applebee's® Signature Barbecue Sauce."

Club House Grill
3 thin deli ham slices
3 thin deli oven-roasted turkey slices
1 thin slice Monterey Jack cheese
1 thin slice cheddar cheese
4 slices bacon, cooked and drained
one layer iceberg lettuce
1 or 2 tomato slices
1 tablespoon butter or margarine
2 slices sourdough bread
mayo
Bull's - Eye® BBQ Sauce, on the side for dipping

Preparation:
Butter both slices of bread. Place deli meat and cheese on one slice each butter side down. Then grill both slices butter side down on low heat until golden brown and cheese melts. Remove from heat. Transfer the meat. Place it on top of the cheese. Place bacon, lettuce and tomato on top of deli

76

meat. Spread mayo on the top slice of bread. Close sandwich and cut in half. Serve with barbecue sauce on the side.

Olive Garden® Chicken Vino Bianco
Copycat Restaurant Recipe
4 servings

Menu Description - "Pan-seared chicken breasts with mushrooms, tomatoes, onions and garlic in a white wine butter sauce over linguine."

Chicken Vino Bianco
2 tablespoons olive oil
4 boneless and skinless chicken breasts
½ cup finely chopped onion
2 garlic cloves, minced
2 cups sliced mushrooms
½ cup white wine
1 cup chopped canned tomatoes, drained
1/4 cup heavy cream
2 tablespoons fresh parsley, chopped
8 ounces linguine

Preparation:
Heat oil in non stick skillet over medium heat. Season chicken breasts with salt and pepper. Brown chicken in hot oil and remove to a plate. Meanwhile, cook linguine according to package directions. Stir in onions and garlic in the same skillet and cook until tender. Stir in mushrooms and cook until golden.
Stir in wine and bring to simmer. Stir in tomatoes and return to a simmer. Season with salt and pepper

and return chicken to pan.
Cook over medium heat until sauce begins to
thicken. Finish sauce with cream and parsley. Serve
warm over linguine pasta.

Applebee's® Grilled Tilapia with Mango Salsa
Copycat Restaurant Recipe
4 servings

Menu Description - "A great catch, this delicately seasoned grilled fish is topped with mango salsa and served over a bed of rice pilaf with steamed vegetables"

Tilapia
4 white fish fillets, such as Tilapia
1 teaspoon Caribbean jerk seasoning
package of rice pilaf
cooking spray

Preparation:
Cook the rice pilaf according to package directions, then divide among four plates. Delicately season both sides of each Tilapia with Caribbean jerk seasoning; coat lightly with cooking spray. Grill. Transfer to plates and top with homemade peach mango salsa or a jar of store - bought peach mango salsa over a bed of rice pilaf.

Mango Salsa
2 cups diced fresh mango
2 cups fresh peaches, pitted and chopped
2 cloves garlic, minced
2 tablespoons chopped fresh ginger root
1/4 cup fresh basil or cilantro, chopped

2 Serrano chile peppers, diced
1/4 cup fresh lime juice

Preparation:
In a large bowl, mix together the mangoes, peaches,
garlic, ginger and basil or cilantro.
Add the chilies and lime juice to taste; mix well.
Allow to chill 2 hours before serving.

Tip: You can find prepared peach - mango salsa in
the gourmet salsa section of your supermarket.

Olive Garden® Chicken Marsala
Copycat Restaurant Recipe
4 servings

Menu Description - "Sautéed chicken breasts in a savory sauce of mushrooms, garlic and marsala wine. Served with Tuscan roasted potatoes and bell peppers."

Chicken Marsala
1/4 cup all-purpose flour
½ teaspoon salt
1/4 teaspoon black pepper
½ teaspoon dried oregano
4 skinless, boneless chicken breast halves
4 tablespoons butter
4 tablespoons olive oil
1 cup sliced mushrooms
½ cup Marsala wine
1 garlic clove, chopped (optional)

Preparation:
In a bowl, mix together the flour, salt, pepper and oregano.
Coat chicken pieces in flour mixture.
In a large skillet, melt butter in oil over medium heat. Saute garlic clove. Place chicken in the pan, and lightly brown.
Turn over chicken pieces, and add mushrooms. Pour in wine. Cover skillet; simmer chicken 10 minutes,

turning once, until no longer pink and juices run clear.

Red Lobster® Fudge Overboard®
Copycat Restaurant Recipe
8 servings

Menu Description - "A warm chocolate-pecan brownie served with vanilla ice cream, topped with chocolate sauce & whipped cream."

Pecan Brownies
13 x 9 family size package of brownie mix
egg (use the fewest number of egg(s) as required by package directions, too many eggs make brownies that taste like cake)
oil according to package directions
½ cup chopped pecans

Preparation:
Follow the directions of the brownie mix, then add ½ cup chopped pecans. Pour mixture into pan. Bake according to package directions.

Chocolate Sauce
4 unsweetened chocolate squares (Baker's®)
½ cup butter
3 cups sugar
1 can (12 ounce) evaporated milk (Carnation®)
½ teaspoon salt

Preparation:
Melt chocolate and butter in a large, heavy

84

saucepan over low heat, stirring constantly. Add sugar, 1 cup at a time, alternately with evaporated milk, beginning and ending with sugar; stir constantly over medium heat 5 minutes or until smooth. Stir in salt.

Whipped Cream
1 can of Reddi whip® whipped cream

Preparation:
You can microwave the brownie and chocolate sauce in separate dishes to make it hot for your dessert. Place a scoop of ice cream over brownie after micro waving. Drizzle hot chocolate sauce over ice cream. Finish by topping with whipped cream.

Benihana® Banana Tempura
Copycat Restaurant Recipe
4 servings

Menu Description - "After a hearty Teppanyaki meal, nothing helps to cleanse the pallet like a banana tempura!"

Banana Tempura
1 egg
1 cup ice water
2 cups flour, divided
vegetable oil
4 bananas
4 scoops of vanilla or strawberry ice cream
½ cup honey (optional)

Preparation:
Heat oil to 375 degrees F in fryer. Heat honey in saucepan or microwave until liquid and hot. Peel the bananas. Cut bananas into 1 inch pieces. Beat egg in a bowl. Add ice water to the bowl. Add one cup flour to the bowl and mix very lightly. Place one cup flour on a plate. Dredge banana pieces in flour; shake off excess. Next, lightly dip banana pieces in batter. Carefully, place in the hot oil and fry until golden, about 2 minutes, turning as they cook. Drain on a rack or paper towels. Place banana pieces in dishes; drizzle with heated honey and serve with your choice of ice cream.

Tip: You can make vegetable and shrimp tempura with the batter and cooking instructions above. Prepare vegetables by cutting into 3/4 of an inch thickness. Cook vegetables first at 340 degrees F until brown. To prepare shrimp make a couple incisions on stomach side of each shrimp so it will stay straight. Pick it up by the tail and dip body into the batter. Then cook shrimp at 350 degrees F until brown. Serve with a tempura dipping sauce, soy sauce or plum sauce.

For more tips on making tempura visit:
www.japanesefood.about.com

The American Cafe® Peanut Butter Ice Cream Pie
Copycat Restaurant Recipe
9 servings

Menu Description - "Our signature peanut butter ice cream pie chock-full of Reese's® peanut butter crumbles in a graham cracker crust with chocolate syrup."

Peanut Butter Ice Cream Pie
Breyers® REESE'S® Peanut Butter Cups™ Ice Cream
15 Reese's® Peanut Butter Cups™
9" Graham Cracker Pie Shell
Hershey's® Chocolate Syrup

Preparation:
First chop 6 Reese's® peanut butter cups™ into crumbles. Scoop ice-cream with a large spoon into pie shell. (If ice-cream is frozen, let it set out for 10 minutes or microwave it for 8 seconds in its container.) Periodically pat down with spoon or spatula. When you are finished filling the pie shell with ice-cream, smooth the top of the pie with a spatula to give it a smooth appearance. Then sprinkle chopped Reese's® crumbles over the pie evenly. Then wedge 9 whole Reese's® peanut butter cups™ into the edge of the pie leaving about a half inch of space between each one. Cover with saran wrap and place in pie container. Freeze. Cut a slice,

place on a plate and drizzle with Hershey's® syrup.
Serve immediately.

None Such Place French Silk Pie
Copycat Restaurant Recipe
6 servings

None Such Place is an upscale restaurant located in Richmond, Virginia.

French Silk Pie
½ cup butter, softened
3/4 cup white sugar
2 squares Bakers® unsweetened chocolate, melted
1 teaspoon vanilla
2 eggs
1 (9 inch) pastry pie shell, baked

Preparation:
Cream butter and sugar in a bowl for mixer. Add melted chocolate and vanilla. Add 1 egg and beat 5 minutes at medium speed in mixer. Add second egg. Beat another 5 minutes. Pour into a cooled baked pie shell and refrigerate.

O'Charley's® Ooey Gooey Caramel Pie
Copycat Restaurant Recipe
9 servings

Menu Description - "Our specialty! Graham cracker crust filled with creamy caramel and topped with whipped topping, chocolate chips and pecans."

Caramel Pie
10 inch graham cracker pie shell
36 individually wrapped caramels, unwrapped
1/4 cup butter
1/4 cup milk
3/4 cup brown sugar
3 eggs
½ teaspoon vanilla extract
1/4 teaspoon salt

Preparation:
Preheat the oven to 350 degrees F. In a medium saucepan, combine caramels, butter and milk. Cook over low heat. Do not stir with a plastic spoon. Stir frequently until mixture is smooth. Remove from heat.
In a large bowl, combine sugar, eggs, vanilla, and salt.
Gradually add the caramel mixture. Stir well.
Pour mixture into pie crust. Bake for 45 minutes. Remove from oven. Refrigerate. Follow next two steps right before serving slices.

Whipped Topping
7 ounce can Reddi whip®

Preparation:
Place a single layer of Reddi whip® topping over each pie slice when it is served. Placing whipped topping on the pie before serving time will result in the whipped topping melting before it is needed.

Toppings
2 tablespoons mini chocolate chips
2 tablespoons pecan chips

Preparation:
Place each topping in separate bowls. Sprinkle each topping over whipped topping evenly and sparingly.

Tip: To slow down the browning of a pie during baking, wrap strips of aluminum foil around the edge of the pie. Use this technique to prevent an extra golden brown crust.

Outback Steakhouse® Sydney's Sinful Sundae®
Copycat Restaurant Recipe
1 serving

Menu Description - "'Ava go at it. Vanilla ice cream rolled in toasted coconut, covered in chocolate sauce and topped with whipped cream."

Sundae
1 cup shredded sweetened coconut, toasted
large scoop vanilla ice cream
2 tablespoons chocolate sauce
2 strawberries
whipped cream

Preparation:
Chill bowl, cream and beaters that you will be using to make whipped cream.
Toast coconut. To toast coconut, spread on shallow cookie sheet and toast in 325 degree F oven for 8 to 10 minutes or until lightly browned, checking often to prevent burning.
Allow to cool completely.
Make chocolate sauce from the Red Lobster® Fudge Overboard® recipe.
Make whipped cream from recipe below when ready to use. Form a large ice cream scoop with an ice cream scooper. Freeze ice cream scoop(s) for 15 minutes if needed. Then roll ice cream scoop in toasted coconut, pressing gently on ice cream.

Freeze coconut - ice cream scoop till ready to use. Place in an ice cream dish. Quarter one strawberry lengthwise; place around ice cream scoop. Heat chocolate sauce in microwave. Drizzle chocolate sauce over ice cream scoop. Place a large portion of whipped cream over ice cream using an ice cream scooper. Place a strawberry on top of dessert.

Whipped Cream
1 cup heavy cream
1/4 cup sugar
1 teaspoon vanilla

Preparation:
Chill the bowl, cream and beaters before starting. Make whipped cream using a mixer on high speed. Whip cream until almost stiff. Add sugar and vanilla; beat until cream holds peaks. Do not over whip. Refrigerate.

Tip: Dollops of whipped cream can be frozen on waxed paper, stored in a container. Thaw dollops before using.

Pantry Note:

Restaurants often times use fresh herbs in their recipes. To duplicate the dishes of restaurants, it's best to use fresh herbs if the recipe calls for them. However, you can substitute dried herbs for fresh if you like. Here's the exchange rate: one tablespoon minced fresh approximately equals one teaspoon dried.

Cookbook Holder:

Simply open your cookbook to the page of your recipe, attach a wooden pants hanger across the top, and hook it on a nearby cabinet doorknob. This saves working space and you won't spill food on your cookbook since it is up and out of the way.